AMAZING ANIMALS

ELK

BY VALERIE BODDEN

CREATIVE EDUCATION • CREATIVE PAPERBACKS

Published by Creative Education and
Creative Paperbacks
P.O. Box 227, Mankato, Minnesota 56002
Creative Education and Creative Paperbacks
are imprints of The Creative Company
www.thecreativecompany.us

Design by The Design Lab
Production by Rachel Klimpel
Art direction by Rita Marshall

Photographs by Alamy (Danita Delimont, Design Pics Inc,
georgesanker.com, Jim Cumming, Maxim Kulko, Michelle
Holihan, robertharding, Robert McGouey/Wildlife),
Dreamstime (Isselee), Getty (Enn Li Photography, Julie
Rideout, THE PALMER), iStock (milehightraveler), Minden
Pictures (Mark Raycroft), National Geographic Creative
(MICHAEL S. QUINTON), Shutterstock (Dimitris Timpilis,
Marilyn D. Lambertz)

Library of Congress Cataloging-in-Publication Data
Names: Bodden, Valerie, author.
Title: Elk / by Valerie Bodden.
Description: Mankato, Minnesota : The Creative Com-
pany, [2023] | Series: Amazing animals | Includes
bibliographical references and index. | Audience: Ages
6–9 | Audience: Grades 2–3 | Summary: "Elementary-
aged readers will discover that male elk use their antlers
to fight. Full color images and clear explanations highlight
the habitat, diet, and lifestyle of these fascinating crea-
tures."– Provided by publisher.
Identifiers: LCCN 2021053399 (print) | LCCN
2021053400 (ebook) | ISBN 9781640265622 (library
binding) | ISBN 9781682771174 (paperback) | ISBN
9781640006812 (ebook)
Subjects: LCSH: Elk–Juvenile literature.
Classification: LCC QL737.U55 R535 2023 (print) |
LCC QL737.U55 (ebook) | DDC 599.65/7–dc23/
eng/20211203
LC record available at https://lccn.loc.gov/2021053399
LC ebook record available at https://lccn.loc.
gov/2021053400

Table of Contents

Rocky Mountain elk are found in the western United States and Canada.

Elk are the second-biggest deer in the world. Only moose are bigger. The **Shawnee** called elk *wapiti.* This means "white rump." Most elk live in western North America.

Shawnee Native American peoples of the eastern and midwestern U.S. who now live mainly in Oklahoma

The thick winter coat and mane fall off in the spring.

In summer, elk have short, reddish fur. They grow two layers of thick fur in winter. The undercoat is short. The tan upper coat is longer. A dark mane grows around the neck. Male elk, or bulls, have **antlers**.

antlers branched, bony growths on the head of an adult male deer

The biggest bulls can weigh 1,000 pounds (454 kg). Females, or cows, are smaller. Elk are fast. They can run 35 miles (56.3 km) per hour.

A bull's antlers fall off at the end of winter and regrow.

Elk move from place to place as they look for food.

Elk live in grasslands and mountains. They **graze** in the morning and evening. In the winter, they move to **valleys** and low forests. Trees block the wind and snow.

graze to feed on grasses growing on the land

valleys low areas of land between mountains or hills, often with a stream or river flowing through them

Elk eat grasses, shrubs, and twigs. They do not have any top front teeth. They use their sharp bottom teeth and hard top gums to rip plants. Elk eat up to 30 pounds (13.6 kg) of food per day.

Elk have a special four-part stomach that breaks down woody food.

Spots on a calf's coat go away by the end of summer.

In late spring, a pregnant cow finds a hidden spot. She gives birth to one **calf.** The newborn calf weighs about 35 pounds (15.9 kg). It stays with its mother for a year.

calf a baby elk

The lighter fur on elk's backsides helps them blend together in a herd.

Elk live in groups called herds. Every winter, several herds join together. This helps keep them safe from **predators** like wolves. Wild elk can live up to 20 years.

predators animals that kill and eat other animals

Bulls sometimes fight. They crash their antlers together. Then they push against each other. The weaker bull usually runs away. Bulls make loud bugling calls, too. These calls can be heard up to a mile (1.6 km) away!

When bulls lock antlers to fight, it is also called sparring.

Many people travel to western North America to see elk in the wild. Others see them in zoos. It is amazing to see these powerful deer in person.

Watch elk from a safe distance—do not call them closer!

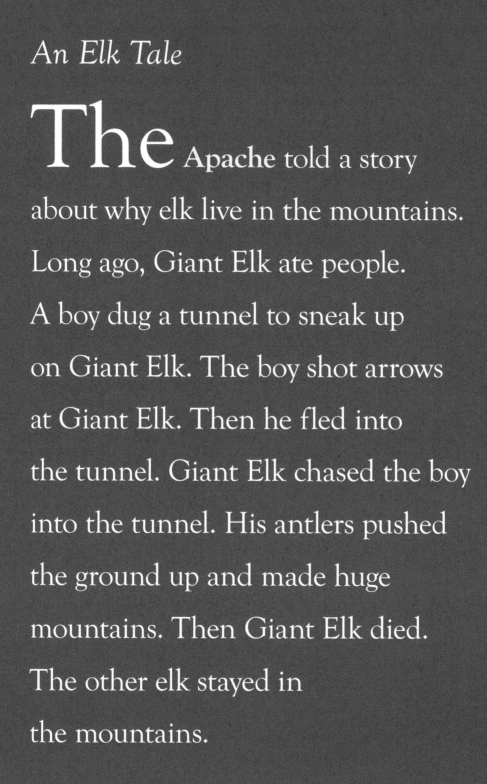

An Elk Tale

The Apache told a story about why elk live in the mountains. Long ago, Giant Elk ate people. A boy dug a tunnel to sneak up on Giant Elk. The boy shot arrows at Giant Elk. Then he fled into the tunnel. Giant Elk chased the boy into the tunnel. His antlers pushed the ground up and made huge mountains. Then Giant Elk died. The other elk stayed in the mountains.

Apache Native American peoples of the southwestern U.S. and northern Mexico

ELK

Read More

Mihaly, Christy. *Rocky Mountain*. Vero Beach: Rourke Educational Media, 2019.

Sterry, Paul. *Deer, Elk & Mountain Goats*. Broomall: Mason Crest, 2019.

Websites

8 Fascinating Facts about Elk
https://www.visitestespark.com/blog/post/8-fascinating-facts-about-elk/
This site has fun facts about elk.

Elk Facts
https://www.rmef.org/elk-facts/
Learn more about elk with videos.

Note: Every effort has been made to ensure that the websites listed above are suitable for children, that they have educational value, and that they contain no inappropriate material. However, because of the nature of the Internet, it is impossible to guarantee that these sites will remain active indefinitely or that their contents will not be altered.

Index